IF THIS ISN'T NICE, WHAT IS?

IF THIS I

'T NICE, WHAT IS?

advice to the young
The graduation speeches

KURT VONNEGUT

selected and introduced by DAN WAKEFIELD

SEVEN STORIES PRESS
New York • Oakland

Electronic edition published 2013, 2014
by RosettaBooks LLC, New York.

Library of Congress Cataloging-in-Publication Data
Vonnegut, Kurt.[Speeches. Selections]
If this isn't nice, what is? : advice for the young /
Kurt Vonnegut ; introduction by Dan Wakefield.
—First Seven Stories Press Edition.
pages cm
Chiefly consists of selected graduation speeches given by
Vonnegut at various educational institutions.
ISBN 978-1-60980-591-3 (hardcover)
I. Wakefield, Dan. II. Title.
PS3572.O5A6 2014
815'.54—dc23
2013050689

Cover and Interior design by Stewart Cauley.
ISBN ePub edition: 9780795333637
Printed in the United States

9 8 7 6 5 4 3 2 1

Publisher's Note: The art by Kurt Vonnegut in *If This Isn't Nice,
What Is?* first appeared in *Breakfast of Champions* in ad hoc fashion.
Here the drawings have been re-imagined and repurposed by
our design team to accompany the author's speeches because
these particular texts and the notebook art of these drawings
seemed to us to strike up intimate conversations with readers
in similar ways. The Kurt Vonnegut Jr Copyright Trust
agreed, and so this rather than some other more eclectic
combination of text and art is what we went with.

Contents

INTRODUCTION
Dan Wakefield

After the publication of his novel *Slaughterhouse-Five* brought him worldwide acclaim in 1969, Kurt Vonnegut became one of America's most popular graduation speakers. Even before that first of many bestsellers was published, Vonnegut had become an underground hero of the youth of the sixties who were hungry for new ways of looking at the world and alternatives to the status quo. College students were passing around dog-eared paperback copies of his earlier novels, such as *Cat's Cradle* and *The Sirens of Titan*, even before *Slaughterhouse-Five* had made him a household name. From his earliest short stories that were published in the popular

weeklies of the nineteen-fifties, including *Colliers* and *The Saturday Evening Post*, Vonnegut's work spoke to young people, and that appeal has never faded. His novels, essays, and stories are taught in colleges and high schools throughout the U.S., and as Prof. Shaun O'Connell at the University of Massachusetts in Boston has told me, "It's hard to get students to read Updike and Bellow anymore, but they still love Vonnegut."

To his own surprise and chagrin, Vonnegut was hailed as a "spokesman" of youth and a hero of the counterculture of the sixties, yet he was, ironically, a "counter-counterculture" figure. He satirized the easy promises to inner and world peace being peddled by the Maharishi Mahesh Yogi in an article for *Esquire* called "Yes, We Have No Nirvanas." As Eastern meditations such as Zen became a fad, Vonnegut maintained that we had our own Western method of achieving the same results of slowing the heartbeat and stilling the mind; it was called "reading short stories." He called this practice "Buddhist Catnaps." He was not, however, one of those adults of the era who found nothing to admire

in the youth culture. He had written that "The function of the artist is to make people like life better than before," and when asked if he'd ever seen that done he answered, "Yes, the Beatles did it."

He also loved the blues, and jazz. He wrote to a friendly literary critic that, "During my childhood in Indianapolis, local jazz musicians excited me and made me happy."

He did not believe drugs had such an effect. In one speech in this collection, he tells his audience: "I've been a coward about heroin and cocaine and LSD and so on. . . . I did smoke a joint of marijuana one time with Jerry Garcia of the Grateful Dead, just to be sociable. It didn't seem to do anything to me, one way or the other, so I never did it again."

Hardly the words of a hippie. One of the well-known hippies of that era, the writer Raymond Mungo, invited me and Vonnegut to visit the commune he started in Brattleboro, Vermont (and later wrote about in his memoir *Total Loss Farm*). He told us that one reason he and his friends wanted to start the commune and learn to "live off the land" in a simple way was that "we want to be the last

people on earth." Vonnegut said, "Isn't that kind of a stuck-up kind of thing to want to be?"

In the way he spoke and the way he wrote, Vonnegut was always coming up with the plain-spoken words and phrases that people thought but didn't say, the ideas that expressed inner feelings, that rattled preconceptions and made you look at things from a different angle. He was the one who pointed out the elephant in the room, the one who saw that the Emperor had no clothes.

That same Raymond Mungo who ushered me and Vonnegut around his commune in 1970 emailed me recently after reading the collection of Vonnegut's letters that I recently edited to say that "Kurt was and remains an important writer and one who will be read beyond all our lifetimes." A new generation of Vonnegut fans was introduced to his work in 2005 when he appeared on *The Daily Show* with Jon Stewart with his last book, *A Man Without a Country*, and teenagers are still moved today by his stories such as *Harrison Bergeron* that are taught in high school classes.

Vonnegut neither wrote down to his readers nor

tried to go over their heads with wisdom. He was playful at the same time as he was profound, and in that same style and spirit he spoke to graduating classes. He did not speak to them as if they were a different, lesser breed because they were young; he disdained generation generalizations. He told one of these graduating classes " . . . we are not members of different generations, as unlike, as some people would have us believe, as Eskimos and Australian Aborigines. We are all so close to each other in time that we should think of ourselves as brothers and sisters. . . . Whenever my children complain about the planet to me, I say 'Shut up! I just got here myself.'" (Vonnegut had three children of his own, and adopted four others, including his last child, Lily, with second wife Jill Krementz.)

Popular as he was as a graduation speaker, Vonnegut never graduated from college. He left Cornell to join the Army in World War II, and the Army sent him to study bacteriology at Butler University and mechanical engineering at Carnegie Tech and the University of Tennessee, then assigned him to the infantry and gave him a rifle. While serving

as an advanced scout for the 106th Infantry in the Battle of the Bulge, he was captured by the Germans and sent to a prisoner of war Camp in Dresden, where he survived the firebombing of that city while quartered in an underground meat locker called Slaughterhouse-Five. When he came home from the war he studied anthropology at the University of Chicago on the G.I. Bill and worked as a reporter for the Chicago News Bureau. Although he completed all the course work for his master's degree, his ideas for a thesis were turned down, and he had to move on to take a job in public relations at General Electric. He was given an honorary degree by the university years later, after he was famous.

"So it goes . . ."

Vonnegut's fame as a writer did not come until he was 47 years old. Before that he struggled to support a large family—not only his wife and their own three children, but three children of his sister who died of cancer at age 41, a day after her husband had been killed when his commuter train crashed off a bridge. The popular weekly magazines of the fifties, whose payments for his short stories enabled Vonnegut to

leave his job at General Electric, died off with the advent of television, and he had to scramble to make a living. He failed to sell a shirt company on his idea for a new kind of bow tie, had no success creating a new board game, opened a dealership for Saab automobiles when they were as yet little known in this country, and when that failed, commuted to Boston to write for an ad agency; he was turned down for a job teaching English at Cape Cod Community College, taught at a school for troubled boys, was turned down for a Guggenheim Fellowship, and through it all, kept writing. He died, in 2007, at the age of 84, still writing.

He was not about to peddle cut-rate formulas for overnight success or blue-sky bromides to young people who sought his advice.

Unlike most graduation speakers, who have a canned speech for all such occasions, simply inserting the name of a new university, Vonnegut brought something freshly minted, coming up with new ideas, new stories, new sources of wit and provocations to think about. He did, however, have certain cherished themes that he managed to work into

almost all his talks—the appreciation of teachers, the importance of noticing and acknowledging the small, sweet moments of everyday life by stopping to say, as his Uncle Alex had taught him, "If this isn't nice, what is?" His messages to graduates were not all sweetness and light by a long shot. There is always his despair at the destruction of the planet, his contempt for the politicians who get us into war from the safety of their age and position, our need for the extended families and puberty ceremonies that gave strength to past societies and whose absence plagues our own.

Vonnegut wrote that "a writer is first and foremost a teacher," and his talks to graduates always taught the lesson that underlies all his work, a lesson, bluntly uttered by a character in one of his early novels, that he passed on to fans who sought his advice: "There's only one rule I know of—Goddam it, you've got to be kind." Coming from a long line of German Freethinkers, Vonnegut was not a Christian, though he spoke of Jesus as "the greatest and most humane of human beings." In a talk he gave at St. Clement Episcopal Church in New York

City ("Palm Sunday"), he said: "I am enchanted by the Sermon on the Mount. Being merciful, it seems to me, is the only good idea we have had so far. Perhaps we will get another good idea by and by—and then we will have two good ideas."

He served as honorary chairman of the American Humanist Society, and explained in one of his talks: "We Humanists behave as honorably as we can without any expectations of rewards or punishments in the afterlife. We serve as best we can the only abstraction with which we have any familiarity, which is our community."

Vonnegut was a staunch believer in serving one's community, wherever or whatever it might be. Although some graduating classes will have a "handful of celebrities" who move on to the national stage, he pointed out that most would find themselves "building or strengthening your communities. Please love that destiny, if it turns out to be yours—for communities are all that's substantial about the world. The rest is hoop-la. And for your footloose generation, that community could as easily be New York City or Washington, Paris or

Houston—or Adelaide, Australia. Or Shanghai or Kuala Lumpur."

Or it might be the city or town where you were born and grew up. Vonnegut and I were both born and grew up in Indianapolis, but left to go off to college and live far away from there. Once while we were walking down the street in New York, Vonnegut turned to me and said, "You know, Dan, we never had to leave home to be writers, because there are people there just as smart and just as dumb, just as kind and just as mean, as anywhere else in the world." He was proud of the education he received at Shortridge High School, where he had worked on our school paper, *The Daily Echo*, as I did a decade later. When asked once by an interviewer, "Where did you get your radical ideas?" he answered proudly and without hesitation, "The public schools of Indianapolis."

Vonnegut took part in the communities he lived in, serving in the Volunteer Fire Department of Alplaus, New York, where he lived while working for General Electric in Schenectady. When he lived in Barnstable, on Cape Cod, Kurt and his

wife Jane conducted a Great Books course for the community. (A Phi Beta Kappa from Swarthmore, Jane had him read *The Brothers Karamazov* on their honeymoon.) When he moved to New York City, he became deeply involved in the PEN Club, serving as vice president and fighting for the rights of writers around the world.

If your destiny was not to live and work in a big city or a foreign land, it was just as important and admirable, in Vonnegut's view, to serve the place where you found yourself and felt yourself fulfilled, no matter how small or obscure that place might seem to the rest of the world. When his friend Jerome Klinkowitz, a teacher and literary critic, asked his advice about moving from a small town in Iowa to a more prestigious position on the East Coast, Vonnegut wrote him, "I am certain you are highly valued and badly needed right where you are. That must be a nourishing situation. If you move East, you may find that life becomes a lot less personal." Klinkowitz heeded his advice to stay where he was, and told me years later, "It was the best advice I ever got."

In his talks, as in his books and stories and essays, Vonnegut conveys what he feels is the message many people "need desperately to receive:"

"I feel and think much as you do, care about many of the things you care about, although most people don't care about them. You are not alone."

While most of the talks here are to graduating classes, one is to the Indiana Civil Liberties Union, and another is an acceptance of the Carl Sandburg Literary Award; what he has to say in both is as relevant to young people as his words to the graduates. They convey the message that he sent to the chairman of the School Board of Drake, North Dakota, who had not only banned his novel *Slaughterhouse-Five*, but for good measure, had burned copies of it in the high school furnace:

" . . . if you were to bother to read my books, to behave as educated persons would, you would learn that they are not sexy, and do not argue in favor of wildness of any kind. They beg that people be kinder and more responsible than they often are. It is true that some of the characters speak coarsely. That is because people speak coarsely in real life.

Especially soldiers and hard-working men speak coarsely, and even our most sheltered children know that. And we all know, too, that those words really don't damage children much. They didn't damage us when we were young. It was evil deeds and lying that hurt us."

You will find no lies in Vonnegut's words of advice. He is one of the truth tellers of our time.

— *Dan Wakefield*

BACCALAUREATE

A show of hands, please:
How many of you have had a teacher
at any stage of your education,
from the first grade until this day in May,
who made you happier to be alive,
prouder to be alive,
than you had previously believed
possible?
Good!
Now say the name of that teacher
to someone
sitting or standing near you.
All done?
Thank you, and drive home safely,
and God bless you all.

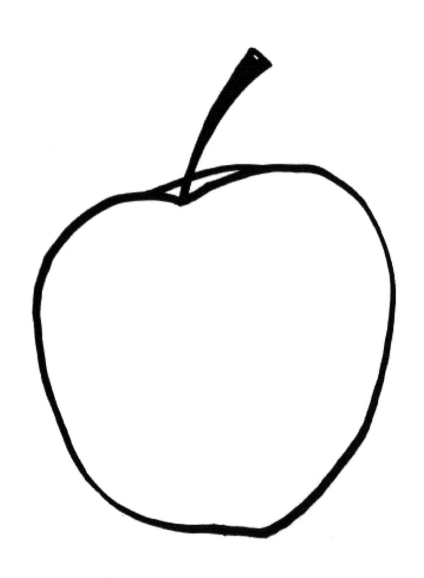

1
HOW TO MAKE MONEY
AND FIND LOVE!

Fredonia College, Fredonia, New York,
May 20, 1978

As if that information weren't enough. Vonnegut explains why
we laugh at jokes, why we are lonely, and why there are really
six seasons in the year instead of only four.

Your class spokesperson has just said that she is
sick and tired of hearing people say, "I'm glad I'm
not a young person these days." All I can say is, "I'm
glad I'm not a young person these days."

Your college's president wished to exclude all
negative thinking from his farewell to you, and so
has asked me to make this announcement: "All per-
sons who still owe parking fees are to pay up before

3

leaving the property, or there will be monkey business with their transcripts."

When I was a boy in Indianapolis, there was a humorist there named Kin Hubbard. He wrote a few lines for *The Indianapolis News* every day. Indianapolis needs all the humorists it can get. He was often as witty as Oscar Wilde. He said, for instance, that prohibition was better than no liquor at all. He said that whoever named near-beer was a poor judge of distance.

I assume that the really important stuff has been spread out over your four years here and that you have no need of anything much from me. This is lucky for me. I have only this to say, basically: this is the end—this is childhood's end for certain. "Sorry about that," as they used to say in the Vietnam War.

Perhaps you have read the novel *Childhood's End* by Arthur C. Clarke, one of the few masterpieces in the field of science fiction. All of the others were written by me. In Clarke's novel, the characters undergo spectacular evolutionary change. The children become very different from the parents, less physical, more spiritual—and one day they form up into a sort of column of light which spirals out into

the universe, its mission unknown. The book ends there. You seniors, however, look a great deal like your parents, and I doubt that you will go radiantly into space as soon as you have your diplomas in hand. It is far more likely that you will go to Buffalo or Rochester or East Quogue—or Cohoes.

And I suppose you will all want money and true love, among other things. I will tell you how to make money: work very hard. I will tell you how to win love: wear nice clothing and smile all the time. Learn the words to all the latest songs.

What other advice can I give you? Eat lots of bran to provide necessary bulk in your diet. The only advice my father ever gave me was this: "Never stick anything in your ear." The tiniest bones in your body are inside your ears, you know—and your sense of balance, too. If you mess around with your ears, you could not only become deaf, but you could also start falling down all the time. So just leave your ears completely alone. They're fine, just the way they are.

Don't murder anybody—even though New York State does not use the death penalty.

That's about it.

One sort of optional thing you might do is to realize there are six seasons instead of four. The poetry of four seasons is all wrong for this part of the planet, and this may explain why we are so depressed so much of the time. I mean, Spring doesn't feel like Spring a lot of the time, and November is all wrong for Fall and so on. Here is the truth about the seasons: Spring is May and June! What could be springier than May and June? Summer is July and August. Really hot, right? Autumn is September and October. See the pumpkins? Smell those burning leaves. Next comes the season called "Locking." That is when Nature shuts everything down. November and December aren't Winter. They're Locking. Next comes Winter, January and February. Boy! Are they ever cold! What comes next? Not Spring. Unlocking comes next. What else could April be?

One more optional piece of advice: if you ever have to give a speech, start with a joke, if you know one. For years I have been looking for the best joke in the world. I think I know what it is. I will tell it to you, but you have to help me. You have to say, "No," when I hold up my hand like this. All right? Don't let me down.

Do you know why cream is so much more expensive than milk?

AUDIENCE: No.

It is because the cows hate to squat on those little bottles.

That is the best joke I know. One time when I worked for the General Electric Company over in Schenectady, I had to write speeches for company officers. I put that joke about the cows and the little bottles in a speech for a vice president. He was reading along, and he had never heard the joke before. He couldn't stop laughing, and he had to be led away from the podium with a nosebleed. I was fired the next day.

How do jokes work? The beginning of each good one challenges you to think. We are such earnest animals. When I asked you about cream, you could not help yourselves. You really tried to think of a sensible answer. Why does a chicken cross the road? Why does a fireman wear red suspenders? Why did they bury George Washington on the side of a hill?

The second part of the joke announces that nobody wants you to think, nobody wants to hear your wonderful answer. You are so relieved to at

last meet somebody who doesn't demand that you
be intelligent. You laugh for joy.

I have in fact designed this entire speech so as to
allow you to be as stupid as you like, without strain,
and without penalties of any kind. I have even
written a ridiculous song for the occasion. It lacks
music, but we are up to our necks in composers.
One is sure to come along. The words go like this:

> Adios to teachers and pneumonia.
> If I find out where the party is,
> I'll telephone ya.
> I love you so much, Sonya,
> That I am going to buy you a begonia.
> You love me, too, doan ya, Sonya?

See—you were trying to guess what the next rhyme
was going to be. Nobody cares how smart you are.

I am being so silly because I pity you so much.
I pity all of us so much. Life is going to be very
tough again, just as soon as this is over. And the
most useful thought we can hold when all hell cuts
loose again is that we are not members of different

generations, as unlike, as some people would have us believe, as Eskimos and Australian Aborigines. We are all so close to each other in time that we should think of ourselves as brothers and sisters.

I have several children—seven, to be exact—too many children for an atheist, certainly. Whenever my children complain about the planet to me, I say, "Shut up! I just got here myself. Who do you think I am—Methuselah? You think I like the news of the day any better than you do? You're wrong."

We are all experiencing more or less the same lifetime now.

What is it the slightly older people want from the slightly younger people? They want credit for having survived so long, and often imaginatively, under difficult conditions. Slightly younger people are intolerably stingy about giving them credit for that.

What is it the slightly younger people want from the slightly older people? More than anything, I think, they want acknowledgement, and without further ado, that they are without question women and men now. Slightly older people are intolerably stingy about making any such acknowledgement.

Therefore, I take it upon myself to pronounce those about to graduate women and men. No one must ever treat them like children again. Neither must they ever act like children—ever again.

This is what is known as a puberty ceremony.

I realize that it is coming a little late, but better late than never. Every primitive society ever studied has had a puberty ceremony, at which former children became unchallengeably women and men. Some Jewish communities still honor this old practice, of course, and benefit from it, in my opinion. But, by and large, ultramodern, massively industrialized societies like ours have decided to do without puberty ceremonies—unless you want to count the issuance of drivers' licenses at the age of 16. If you want to count that as a puberty ceremony, then it has a highly unusual feature: a judge can take your puberty away again, even if you're as old as I am.

Another event in the lives of American and European males which might be considered a puberty ceremony is war. If a male comes home from a war, especially with serious wounds, everybody agrees: here indeed is a man. When I came home to Indianapolis from the Second World War in Germany, an uncle of

mine said to me, "By golly—you look like a man now."
I wanted to strangle him. If I had, he would have been
the first German I'd killed. I was a man before I went
to war, but he was damned if he would say so.

I suggest to you that the withholding of a puberty
ceremony from young males in our society is a scheme,
devised cunningly but subconsciously, to make those
males eager to go to war, no matter how terrible or
unjust a war may be. There are just wars, too, of course.
The war I was eager to go to happened to be a just one.

And when does a female stop being a little girl and
become a woman, with all the rights and privileges
appertaining thereto? We all know the answer in our
bones: when she has a baby in wedlock, of course. If
she has that first baby out of wedlock, she is still a child.
What could be simpler or more natural and more obvi-
ous than that—or, in these days and in this society, at
least, more unjust, irrelevant, and just plain stupid?

I think we had better, for our own safety, rein-
state puberty ceremonies.

I not only pronounce those about to graduate as
women and men. With all the powers vested in me, I
pronounce them Clarks as well. Most of you know, I'm

sure, that all white people named Clark are descended from inhabitants of the British Isles who were remarkable for being able to read and write. A black person named Clark, of course, would be descended, most likely, from someone who was forced to work without pay or rights of any kind by a white person named Clark. An interesting family—the Clarks.

I realize that you graduates are all specialized in some way. But you have spent most of the past sixteen or more years learning to read and write. People who can do those things well, as you can, are miracles and, in my opinion, entitle us to suspect that we may be civilized after all. It is terribly hard to learn to read and write. It takes simply forever. When we scold our schoolteachers about the low reading scores of their students, we pretend that it is the easiest thing in the world: to teach a person to read and write. Try it sometime, and you will discover that it is nearly impossible.

What good is being a Clark, now that we have computers and movies and television? Clarking, a wholly human enterprise, is sacred. Machinery is not. Clarking is the most profound and effective

form of meditation practiced on this planet, and far surpasses any dream experienced by a Hindu on a mountaintop. Why? Because Clarks, by reading well, can think the thoughts of the wisest and most interesting human minds throughout all history. When Clarks meditate, even if they themselves have only mediocre intellects, they do it with the thoughts of angels. What could be more sacred than that?

So much for puberty and Clarking. Only two major subjects remain to be covered: loneliness and boredom. No matter what age any of us is now, we are going to be bored and lonely during what remains of our lives.

We are so lonely because we don't have enough friends and relatives. Human beings are supposed to live in stable, like-minded, extended families of fifty people or more.

Your class spokesperson mourned the collapse of the institution of marriage in this country. Marriage is collapsing because our families are too small. A man cannot be a whole society to a woman, and a woman cannot be a whole society to a man. We try, but it is scarcely surprising that so many of us go to pieces.

So I recommend that everybody here join all sorts of organizations, no matter how ridiculous, simply to get more people in his or her life. It does not matter much if all the other members are morons. Quantities of relatives of any sort are what we need.

As for boredom: Friedrich Wilhelm Nietzsche, a German philosopher who died seventy-eight years ago, had this to say: "Against boredom even the gods contend in vain." We are supposed to be bored. It is a part of life. Learn to put up with it, or you will not be what I have declared the members of this graduating class to be: mature women and men.

I come to a close now by noting that the press, whose business is to know and understand everything, often find young people to be apathetic (especially when pundits and commentators can't think of anything else to write about or talk about). The new generation of graduates has failed to eat a certain vitamin or mineral perhaps, iron perhaps. They have tired blood. They need Geritol. Well, as a member of a zippier generation, with sparkle in its eyes and a snap in its stride, let me tell you what kept us as high as kites a lot of the time: hatred.

All my life I've had people to hate—from Hitler to Nixon, not that those two are at all comparable in their villainy. It is a tragedy, perhaps, that human beings can get so much energy and enthusiasm from hate. If you want to feel ten feet tall and as though you could run a hundred miles without stopping, hate beats pure cocaine any day. Hitler resurrected a beaten, bankrupt, half-starved nation with hatred and nothing more. Imagine that.

So it seems quite likely to me that young people of today in the United States of America are not in fact apathetic, but only look that way to people who are used to getting their ecstasies from hatred, among other things, of course. The members of your graduating class are not sleepy, are not listless, are not apathetic. They are simply performing the experiment of doing without hate. Hate is the missing vitamin or mineral or whatever in their diet, they have sensed correctly that hate, in the long run, is about as nourishing as cyanide. This is a very exciting thing they are doing, and I wish them well.

2
ADVICE TO GRADUATING WOMEN (THAT ALL MEN SHOULD KNOW!)

Agnes Scott College, Decatur, Georgia,
May 15, 1999

In which the author answers the question that Freud asked,
but never could figure out: "What do women want?" For good
measure, he also reveals what men really want.

We love you, are proud of you, expect good things from you, and wish you well.

This is a long-delayed puberty ceremony. You are at last officially full-grown women—what you were biologically by the age of 15 or so. I am as sorry as I can be that it took so much time and money before you could at last be licensed as grown-ups.

17

Kin Hubbard, a newspaper humorist in my hometown of Indianapolis when I was growing up, wrote a joke a day for *The Indianapolis News*. One day, I remember, he said, "It's no disgrace to be poor, but it might as well be." He said this about graduation addresses: "I think it would be better if colleges spread out the really important stuff over four years, instead of saving it all up for the very end."

But that's what you're going to get from me: all the really important stuff at the very end.

I am so smart I know what is wrong with the world. Everybody asks during and after our wars, and the continuing terrorist attacks all over the globe, "What's gone wrong?"

What has gone wrong is that too many people, including high school kids and heads of state, are obeying the Code of Hammurabi, a King of Babylonia who lived nearly four thousand years ago. And you can find his code echoed in the Old Testament, too. Are you ready for this?

"An eye for an eye and a tooth for a tooth."

A categorical imperative for all who live in obedience to the Code of Hammurabi, which includes heroes of every cowboy show and gangster show you

ever saw, is this: Every injury, real or imagined, shall be avenged. Somebody's going to be really sorry.

(Horrible laugh.)

Bombs away—or whatever.

When Jesus Christ was nailed to a cross, he said, "Forgive them, Father, they know not what they do." What kind of a man was that? Any real man, obeying the Code of Hammurabi, would have said, "Kill them, Dad, and all their friends and relatives, and make their deaths slow and painful."

His greatest legacy to us, in my humble opinion, consists of only twelve words. They are the antidote to the poison of the Code of Hammurabi, a formula almost as compact as Albert Einstein's "$E = mc^2$."

Jesus of Nazareth told us to say these twelve words when we prayed: "Forgive us our trespasses as we forgive those who trespass against us."

Bye-bye, Code of Hammurabi.

And for those words alone, he deserves to be called "the Prince of Peace."

Every act of war, every act of violence, even by a paranoid schizophrenic, celebrates Hammurabi and shows contempt for Jesus Christ.

Is anybody here a Presbyterian?

I want to warn you: Many people have been burned alive in public for believing what you believe. So watch your backs after you get out of here.

Some of you may know that I am a Humanist, or Freethinker, as were my parents and grand-parents and great grandparents—and so not a Christian. By being a Humanist, I am honoring my mother and father, which the Bible tells us is a good thing to do.

But I say with all my American ancestors, "If what Jesus said was good, and so much of it was absolutely beautiful, what does it matter if he was God or not?"

If Christ hadn't delivered the Sermon on the Mount, with its message of mercy and pity, I wouldn't want to be a human being.

I would just as soon be a rattlesnake.

Revenge provokes revenge which provokes revenge which provokes revenge—forming an unbroken chain of death and destruction linking nations of today to barbarous tribes of thousands and thousands of years ago.

We may never dissuade leaders of our nation or any other nation from responding vengefully, violently, to every insult or injury. In this, the Age of Television, they will continue to find irresistible the temptation to become entertainers, to compete with movies by blowing up bridges and police stations and factories and so on.

Fires, explosions. Come look. Oh my gosh—hey wow.

To quote the late Irving Berlin: "There's no business like show business."

But in our personal lives, our inner lives, at least, we can learn to live without the sick excitement, without the kick of having scores to settle with this particular person, or that bunch of people, or that particular institution or race or nation.

And we can then reasonably ask forgiveness for our trespasses, since we forgive those who trespass against us. And we can teach our children and then our grandchildren to do the same—so that they, too, can never be a threat to anyone.

OK?

Amen.

Not that there hasn't been a lot of good news,

along with the bad, long before you got here. I am talking about the birth of works of art. Music, paintings. Statues, buildings, poems, stories, plays, and essays, and movies (you bet), and humane ideas—which make us feel honored to be members of the human race.

What can you yourselves contribute? You've come this far anyway, and it wasn't easy. And I now recite a famous line by the poet Robert Browning, with one small change. I have replaced his word "man," which in his time was taken to mean "human being," with the word "woman."

May I say, too, that his wife Elizabeth Barrett was as great a poet as he was: "How do I love thee? Let me count the ways . . ." and so on.

While I'm at it, get a load of this: The atomic bomb which we dropped on the people of Hiroshima was first envisioned by a woman, not a man. She was, of course, Mary Wollstonecraft Shelley. She didn't call it an "atomic bomb." She called it "the monster of Frankenstein."

But back to Robert Browning, and what he said about anyone who hopes to make the world better.

Again, I've changed his word "man" to "woman" for this occasion:

"A woman's reach should exceed her grasp, or what's a heaven for?"

And of course the original: "A man's reach should exceed his grasp, or what's a heaven for?"

Sigmund Freud said he didn't know what women wanted. I am so smart I not only know what is wrong with the world, the Code of Hammurabi, but I know what women want. Women want a whole lot of people to talk to. What do they want to talk about? They want to talk about everything.

Men want a lot of pals—and they don't want people to get mad at them.

Some of you may become psychologists or ministers. In either case, you are going to have to deal with men, women, and children whose lives are being damaged by our country's astronomical divorce rate. You should know that when a husband and wife fight, it may seem to be about money or sex or power.

But what they're really yelling at each other about is loneliness. What they're really saying is, "You're not enough people."

Back when most human beings lived in extended families and lived in the same part of the world for the whole of their lives, a marriage was really something to celebrate. Wedding guests laughed instead of cried. The groom was going to get a lot of new pals, and the bride was going to get a whole new bunch of people to talk to about everything.

Nowadays, most of us when we marry get just one person—and, oh sure, maybe a few scruffy in-laws, ready to kill each other, and living hundreds of miles away, if you're lucky—in someplace like Vancouver, British Columbia, or Hollywood, Florida.

So again: If any of you educated people find yourselves in a therapeutic situation vis-à-vis a marriage on the rocks, please realize that the real problem may not be money or sex or power or how to raise a kid. The real trouble with the wife, as far as the husband is concerned, may be that she isn't enough people. The real trouble with the husband, as far as the wife is concerned, may be that he isn't enough people.

If you determine that that really is what they've been yelling at each other about, tell them to

become more people for each other by joining a synthetic extended family—like the Hell's Angels, perhaps, or the American Humanist Association, with headquarters in Amherst, New York—or the nearest church.

I met a man in Nigeria one time, an Ibo who had six hundred relatives he knew quite well. His wife had just had a baby, the best possible news in any extended family.

They were going to take it to meet all its relatives, Ibos of all ages and sizes and shapes. It would even meet other babies, cousins not much older than it was. Everybody who was big enough and steady enough was going to get to hold it, cuddle it, gurgle to it, and say how pretty it was, or handsome.

Wouldn't you have loved to be that baby?

Here is a fact: this wonderful speech is already more than twice as long as the most efficient, effective oration in American history, Abraham Lincoln's address on the battlefield at Gettysburg.

As I speak, the very air we breathe is vibrant with words and images from CNN. In the early days of radio, I remember, people living too close to the

transmitter of KDKA in Pittsburgh used to receive soap operas in their bedsprings and bridgework.

And nowadays, surely, TV is such a pervasive part of so many Americans' lives that they might as well be hearing Wolf Blitzer in their bedsprings and bridgework. And I have a son-in-law who has been swallowed by his computer. He disappeared into it, and I'm not sure we can ever get him back out again. And he has a wife and kids!

There was a time when a graduation speaker, looking out at a sea of beauty and innocence such as this one, would warn you about all the sewer rats you will meet as you flow out of here and into the gutters of the real world. I mean lascivious, untruthful men, tinhorn Casanovas and sociopathic Lochinvars. But *Cosmopolitan* and *Elle* magazines have told you all about them—and told you how to protect yourselves.

If somebody says he loves you, check it out.

And your State and Federal Governments, thank goodness, have told you not to smoke cigarettes, which are evil incarnate. . . . Who in his or her right mind doesn't hate evil with a passion?

Cigarettes are very bad for you—but cigars are very good for you. Cigars are so healthful that there is a magazine devoted to them, with pictures of cigar-smoking celebrities on the cover.

Cigars, of course, are made of trail mix—of nuts and raisins and granola. Why don't you all eat a cigar at bedtime tonight?

No cholesterol.

Firearms are also good for you. No fat, no nicotine, and no cholesterol.

Ask your Congressperson if this isn't true.

And God bless the State and Federal Governments for taking such good care of the public health.

I hope you know that television and computers are no more your friends, and no more increasers of your brainpower, than slot machines. All they want is for you to sit still and buy all kinds of junk, and play the stock market as though it were a game of blackjack.

And only well-informed, warm-hearted people can teach others things they'll always remember and love. Computers and TV don't do that.

A computer teaches a child what a computer can become.

An educated human being teaches a child what a child can become.

Bad men just want your bodies. TVs and computers want your money, which is even more disgusting. It's so much more dehumanizing!

Given a choice, wouldn't you rather have somebody like your body more than your money?

Forbes magazine asked me recently what my favorite technologies were, and I said a corner mailbox, my address book, and the *Encyclopedia Britannica*. The *Britannica* is arranged alphabetically, so you can find out all kinds of stuff, if you know your ABCs.

And putting a letter in a corner mailbox is like feeding a great big bullfrog painted blue.

I thank you for becoming educated. By becoming reasonable and informed persons, you have made this a more rational world than it was before you got here. I give you my word of honor that you graduates are near the very top of the best news I ever heard. By working so hard at becoming wise and reasonable and well-informed, you have made our little planet, our precious little moist, blue-green ball, a saner place than it was before you got here.

Thanks, and God bless those who made it possible for you to improve your minds and souls in the company of students from every part of this country, and foreign nations besides.

What fun, eh? I should say.

Most of you are preparing to enter fields unattractive to greedy persons, such as education and the healing arts. Teaching, may I say, is the noblest profession of all in a democracy.

Some of you will become mothers. I don't recommend it, but these things happen.

If that should fall to your lot, you may find compensation in these words by the poet William Ross Wallace: "The hand that rocks the cradle rules the world."

And keep that kid the hell away from computers and TV sets, unless you want it to be a lonesome imbecile, who steals money from your purse so it can buy stuff.

Don't give up on books. They feel so good—their friendly heft. The sweet reluctance of their pages when you turn them with your sensitive fingertips. A large part of our brains is devoted to deciding whether what our hands are touching is good or bad

for us. Any brain worth a nickel knows books are good for us.

And don't try to make yourself an extended family out of ghosts on the Internet.

Get yourself a Harley and join the Hell's Angels instead.

Every graduation pep talk I've ever given has ended with words about my father's kid brother, Alex Vonnegut, a Harvard educated insurance agent in Indianapolis, who was well-read and wise.

The first graduation at which I spoke, incidentally, was at what was then a women's college—Bennington, in Vermont. The Vietnam War was going on, and the graduates wore no make-up, to show how ashamed and sad they were.

But about my Uncle Alex, who is up in Heaven now. One of the things he found objectionable about human beings was that they so rarely noticed it when they were happy. He himself did his best to acknowledge it when times were sweet. We could be drinking lemonade in the shade of an apple tree in the summertime, and Uncle Alex would interrupt the conversation to say, "If this isn't nice, what is?"

So I hope that you will do the same for the rest of your lives. When things are going sweetly and peacefully, please pause a moment, and then say out loud, "If this isn't nice, what is?"

Let that be the motto of your class: "If this isn't nice, what is?"

That's one favor I've asked of you. Now I ask for another one. I ask it not only of the graduates, but of everyone here, parents and teachers as well. I'll want a show of hands after I ask this question.

How many of you have had a teacher at any level of your education who made you more excited to be alive, prouder to be alive, than you had previously believed possible?

Hold up your hands, please.

Now take down your hands and say the name of that teacher to someone else and tell them what that teacher did for you.

All done?

If this isn't nice, what is?

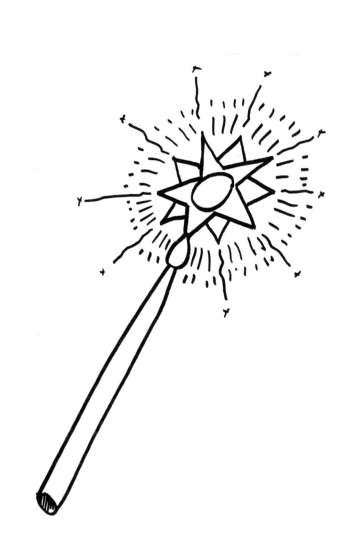

3
HOW TO HAVE SOMETHING
MOST BILLIONAIRES DON'T

Rice University, Houston, Texas,
October 12, 2001

And learn to love your destiny!

Hello.

I have not calculated how much your diplomas cost in time and money. Whatever those ballpark figures are, they surely deserve this reaction from me today: Wow. Wow. Wow.

Thank you, and God bless you and those who made it possible for you to study at an American university. By becoming informed and reasonable

and capable adults, you have made this a better world than it was before you got here.

Have we met before? No. But I have thought a lot about people like you. You men here are Adam. You women are Eve. Who hasn't thought a lot about Adam and Eve?

This is Eden, and you're about to be kicked out. Why? You ate the knowledge apple. It's in your tummies now.

And who am I? I used to be Adam. But now I am Methuselah.

So what does this Methuselah have to say to you, since he has lived so long? I'll pass on to you what another Methuselah said to me. He's Joe Heller, author, as you know, of *Catch-22*. We were at a party thrown by a multi-billionaire out on Long Island, and I said, "Joe, how does it make you feel to realize that only yesterday our host probably made more money than *Catch-22*, one of the most popular books of all time, has grossed worldwide over the past forty years?"

Joe said to me, "I have something he can never have."

I said, "What's that, Joe?"

And he said, "The knowledge that I've got enough."

His example may be of comfort to many of you Adams and Eves, who in later years will have to admit that something has gone terribly wrong—and that, despite the education you received here, you have somehow failed to become billionaires.

Well-dressed people ask me sometimes, with their teeth bared, as though they were about to bite me, if I believe in a redistribution of wealth. I can only reply that it doesn't matter what I think, that wealth is already being redistributed every hour, often in ways that are absolutely fantastic.

Nobel Prizes are peanuts when compared with what a linebacker for the Cowboys makes in a single season nowadays.

For about a hundred years now, the most lucrative prize for a person who made a really meaningful contribution to the culture of the world as a physicist, a chemist, a physiologist, a physician, a writer, or, God bless him or her, a maker of peace, has been the Nobel Prize. It is about a million dollars now. Those dollars come, incidentally, from

a fortune made by a Swede who mixed clay with
nitroglycerine and gave us dynamite.

KABOOM!

Alfred Nobel intended that his prizes make the
planet's most valuable inhabitants independently
wealthy, so that their work could not be inhibited or
bent this way or that way by powerful politicians or
wealthy patrons.

But one million dollars is only a white chip
now—in the worlds of sports and entertainment, on
Wall Street, in many lawsuits, as compensation for
executives of our larger corporations.

One million dollars in the tabloids and on the
evening news is "chump change" now.

I am reminded of a scene in a W. C. Fields movie,
in which he is watching a poker game in a saloon in
a gold-rush town. Fields announces his presence by
putting a one-hundred-dollar bill on the table. The
players barely look up from the game. One of them
finally says, "Give him a white chip."

But the cost of a college education, a minor frac-
tion of a million dollars, is anything but chump
change to most Americans. Have academic degrees

been a way to become famous and rich in the past? In a few cases. You can no doubt name a handful of celebrities who came from here. But most graduates, any place you care to name, have been of use locally rather than nationally, and have commonly been rewarded with modest amounts of money or fame—or sometimes, more's the pity, with utterly undeserved ingratitude.

In time, this will prove to have been the destiny of most, but not all of you. You will find yourselves building or strengthening your communities. Please love that destiny, if it turns out to be yours—for communities are all that's substantial about the world.

All the rest is hoop-la.

And for your footloose generation, that community could as easily be New York City or Washington, D.C., or Paris, or Houston—or Adelaide, Australia, or Shanghai, or Kuala Lumpur.

Mark Twain, at the end of a profoundly meaningful life, for which he never received a Nobel Prize, asked himself what it was we all lived for. He came up with six words which satisfied him. They satisfy me, too. They should satisfy you:

"The good opinion of our neighbors."

Neighbors are people who know you, can see you, can talk to you—to whom you may have been of some help or beneficial stimulation. They are not nearly as numerous as the fans, say, of Madonna or Michael Jordan.

To earn their good opinions, you should apply the special skills you have learned in college, and meet the standards of decency and honor and fair play set by exemplary books and elders.

It's even money that one of you will get a Nobel Prize. Wanna bet? It's only a million bucks, but what the heck. That's better than a sharp stick in the eye, as they say.

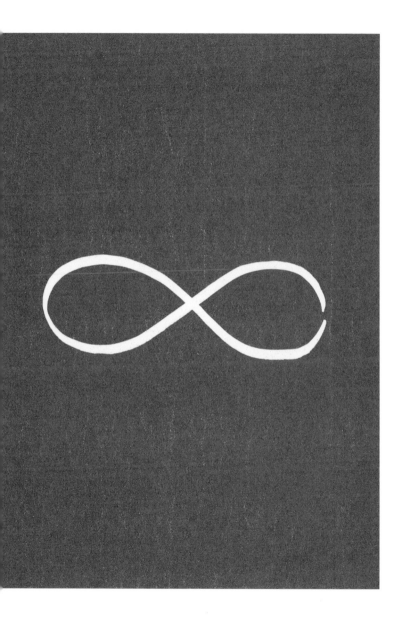

4

WHY YOU CAN'T STOP ME FROM SPEAKING ILL OF THOMAS JEFFERSON

The Indiana Civil Liberties Union

(now The American Civil Liberties Union of Indiana),

Indianapolis, Indiana,

September 6, 2000

Vonnegut tells why the Bill of Rights is "more than just a bunch of amendments," but protects our most important liberties—like freedom of speech, and a lot more. He supports the Second Amendment and explains how "man-killing devices and live ammunition" can best serve us.

There is something you are entitled to know about me—something I'm not proud to confess. This is it: I was born into a society as segregated as Biloxi, Mississippi, except for the drinking fountains and the buses. And I am the product of a lily-white public high school in Indianapolis. It had a faculty worthy of a university. Our teachers there, again lily-white, weren't just teachers. They were their subjects. Our

chemistry teachers were first and foremost chemists. Our physics teachers were first and foremost physicists. Our teacher of ancient history, who was Minnie Lloyd, should have been wearing medals for all she did at the Battle of Thermopylae. Our English teachers were very commonly serious writers. One of mine, the late Marguerite Young, went on to write the definitive biography of Indiana's own Eugene Victor Debs, the middle-class labor leader and socialist candidate for President of the United States, who died in 1926, when I was 4. Millions voted for Debs when he ran for President.

I never met Debs, but I was old enough after World War II to have lunch in this city with another middle-class Indiana labor leader. He was Powers Hapgood. Although he was a Harvard graduate and from a well-to-do family of business people, Powers Hapgood worked as a coal miner to get close, both spiritually and physically, to those he wished to help to help themselves. He then became an officer in the CIO here in Indianapolis.

Not long after our lunch, there was some kind of dust-up on a picket line, and he landed in court as

a witness. The judge, Judge Claycomb, in fact the father of my Shortridge classmate Moon Claycomb, knew of Hapgood's history, and interrupted the proceedings to ask why such a privileged person would spend his life as he had. And Powers Hapgood replied: "Why, the Sermon on the Mount, sir."

And if I am asked why anybody should support their local and national Civil Liberties Unions, I will say that it takes a powerful private organization to compel those who govern us to not violate the crystal clear laws in the Bill of Rights, just as we would not want them to drive when drunk or park by a fireplug. Given the humane and fair and merciful intent of the Bill of Rights, what I would actually be saying, though, subliminally, is, "The Sermon on the Mount, sir or madam."

If you don't know what the Sermon on the Mount is, ask your kid's computer. If you don't know what the laws in the Bill of Rights are, look 'em up, look 'em up. And yes, I know about the Second Amendment, and I'm for it. It doesn't say people who disagree with a president should shoot him, which is what John Wilkes Booth and Lee

Harvey Oswald did. It says in effect that civil-
ians interested in playing with man-killing devices
and live ammunition can best serve the rest of us
in the National Guard, as long as they don't shoot
unarmed college students.[1]

To come back to my lily-white high school, which
had a daily paper. It had such a stunning faculty
because the Great Depression was going on, so
teaching was a plum job for some of the smartest
men in town. But even before the stock market crash
of 1929, when I was 7, it had great teachers because
teaching high school was virtually the only way bril-
liant and informed women could make effective use
of their warmth and intellectual enthusiasm and gift-
edness. Most of my best teachers were women and,
holy smokes, were they ever bright.

Why were women barred then from so many
jobs they now hold with distinction? Because of
what was then believed to be a law of Nature, a
Natural Law. Otherwise, why would Nature have

1 Four unarmed students at Kent State University were shot
and killed by Ohio National Guardsmen on May 4, 1970, while
protesting against the bombing of Cambodia.

made women such lousy fighters? Most of 'em,
with a very few strikingly unattractive exceptions,
couldn't fight their way out of a paper bag.

Why were there no African Americans in my
high school?

African Americans had their own high school, of
course. It was Crispus Attucks. And because of the
peculiar name of our black high school, people of
all colors in Indianapolis were unusual Americans
for knowing who Crispus Attucks was. He was
an African American free man, not a slave, who
stopped a British bullet at the Boston Massacre
in 1770, only six years before our nation became a
beacon of liberty for the whole wide world. In one
book of mine, I nicknamed Crispus Attucks High
School "Innocent Bystander High."

Again: Why were there no African Americans in
Shortridge High School? Because of what was then
believed to be a law of Nature, a Natural Law. Nature
had obviously color-coded people for a reason. Other-
wise, what the hell were all these different colors for?

And why was Thomas Jefferson, possibly the
most beloved of our founding fathers after George

Washington, able to write "all men are created equal," while meaning only white males, not women, God knows, and while owning slaves? Because of what was then believed to be a law of Nature. Jefferson's slaves were mortgaged, by the way. What a shame that you can no longer take the cleaning lady, along with the saxophone, down to the hock shop, if you're short on cash. Those were sure the good old days.

In quite a few ways though, it was still the good old days for white males when I was growing up. I could still feel superior, even in the view of law-enforcement agencies, to half my own race and one hundred percent of all the others. That was comforting! Not only that, but I could get away with all kinds of crap because I was from a good family. But that's another story.

In our all-white sandlot football games, I remember—"Jeffersonian games," you might call them—the ad hoc captain of the side preparing to kick off would call out. "Are you ready, Crispus Attucks?" And the captain of the receivers would inevitably

reply, "We are ready, Ladywood."[2] Come to think of it, that "Ladywood" business had an anti-Catholic ring to it. Come to think of it, we were not only male and white, but also Protestant. So that "Ladywood" insult was a kind of two-fer.

If I have offended some of you by speaking ill of Thomas Jefferson, tough titty for you. I can say anything I please, short of shouting "Fire!" if there is no fire, because I am a citizen of the U.S.A. Your government does not exist and should not exist in order to keep you or anybody else, no matter what color, no matter what race, no matter what religion, from getting your damn fool feelings hurt.

If you found an official powerful enough and dumb enough to actually shut me up about Thomas Jefferson, the two of you would be hauled into court, and the Indiana Civil Liberties Union would make you both feel like something the cat drug in.

Which brings us to Saint Thomas Aquinas, a great Italian theologian and philosopher who eight hundred years ago perceived a hierarchy of laws

2 Ladywood was a Catholic girls' school in Indianapolis.

which human beings should obey. At the top were
God's Laws, from the Old and New Testaments, of
course. Below them were Natural Laws, the ways
Nature, obviously, to both Saint Thomas and Jef-
ferson, expected things to go. Lowest of all were
man's laws. If you think of laws arranged in that
order in a deck of cards, God's Laws would be the
aces, Nature's law would be the kings, and ACLU
lawyers, attempting to secure the civil rights of the
deuces and treys and even unpopular tens and jacks
in our society, would have nothing but pipsqueak
queens to play. I in fact once heard a man dis-
miss the Bill of Rights as "nothing but a bunch of
amendments." Chickenfeed, when compared with
God and Nature.

And indeed the unambiguous laws in the Bill
of Rights might as well have been chickenfeed, or
even chicken droppings, so cruelly spotty was their
enforcement until the start of the lifetimes of people
my age—people born in 1922. Only a year before
we were born were female citizens allowed to vote
and run for office. My Lord! And for many years
after that, until the end of World War II, for Heav-

en's sakes, African American citizens of both sexes were in many parts of the country, this beacon of liberty, discouraged from voting by a combination of technicalities and sheer terror. Don't forget: nobody had ever been punished for lynching one. "Nature red in tooth and claw."[3]

Who were and are the bleeding hearts who fought and fight to make our governments, local, state and federal, behave justly and mercifully and respectfully toward all its citizens, no matter how socially and politically powerless and unpopular they may be? I have an old and once-despised name for them which may surprise you. They are "Abolitionists." We are Abolitionists. Abolition of what? Of human slavery. Such passions for human rights as we have derive their strength from inherited guilt about the unspeakably hideous crime on which so much of the early and even present wealth of the whole of this nation, under God, is based, the labor of kidnapped persons, of slaves. And

3 "Nature red in tooth and claw" is a quote from John Milton's poem "In Memoriam," and refers to predatory animals baring their teeth and claws with the blood of the prey they killed.

we tonight are also atoning as best we can for the murders of brothers by brothers, so to speak, in our Civil War. "Mine eyes have seen the glory of the coming of the Lord. He is trampling out the vineyards where the grapes of wrath are stored."

What did *The Battle Hymn of the Republic* and *Uncle Tom's Cabin* and Lincoln's Gettysburg Address and all that have to do with our present enthusiasm for women's rights? Not that much, really. Women just got lucky this time.

5
HOW MUSIC CURES OUR ILLS
(AND THERE ARE LOTS OF THEM)

Eastern Washington University, Spokane, Washington,
April 17, 2004

Vonnegut looks on the dark side, and finds that music, waltz-
ing, the blues, humor, and "people who behave compassion-
ately" make life worthwhile.

I was so innocent once that I still considered it possible that we could become the humane and reasonable America so many members of my generation used to dream of. We dreamed of such an America during the Great Depression, when there were no jobs. And then we fought and often died for that dream during the Second World War, when there was no peace.

But I know now that there is not a chance in hell of America's becoming humane and reasonable. That is because power corrupts us, and absolute power corrupts us absolutely. Human beings are chimpanzees who get crazy drunk on power. I myself have experienced that intoxication. I was once a Corporal.

By saying our leaders are power-drunk chimpanzees, am I in danger of wrecking the morale of our men and women fighting and dying in the Middle East? Their morale, like so many of their bodies, is already shot to pieces. They are being treated, as I never was, like toys a rich kid got for Christmas.

But I will say this:

No matter how corrupt and greedy our government and our corporations and our media and Wall Street and our religious and charitable organizations may become, the music will still be perfectly wonderful.

If I should ever die, God forbid, let this be my epitaph:

THE ONLY PROOF HE NEEDED OF THE EXISTENCE OF GOD WAS MUSIC.

And I have arranged for a Strauss waltz to be

played as you depart, so you can waltz the heck out of here when it is time to go. For those of you who don't know how to waltz, nothing could be easier and more human. You go step, slide, rest, step, slide, rest, step, slide, rest. Oom, pah, pah, oom, pah, pah.

Bill Gates doesn't seem to realize that we are dancing animals.

During our catastrophically idiotic war in Vietnam, the music just kept getting better and better. We lost that war, by the way. Order couldn't be restored in Indochina until the locals could finally kick us the hell out of there.

That war only made billionaires out of millionaires. This war[4] is making trillionaires out of billionaires. I call that progress.

And how come the people in countries we invade can't fight like ladies and gentlemen, in uniforms, and with tanks and helicopter gunships?

About music: I like Strauss and Mozart and all that, but I would be remiss not to mention the absolutely priceless gift which African Americans gave

4 The first Iraq War.

to the whole wide world when they were still in slavery. I mean the blues. All pop music today, jazz, swing, bebop, Elvis Presley, the Beatles, the Stones, rock 'n' roll, hip-hop, and on and on is derived from the blues.

How do I know it's a gift to the world? One of the best rhythm-and-blues combos I ever heard was three guys and a girl from Finland, playing in a club in Krakow, Poland.

The wonderful writer Albert Murray, who is a jazz historian among other things, told me that, during the era of slavery in this country, an atrocity from which we can never fully recover, the suicide rate per capita among slave owners was much higher than the suicide rate among slaves. Al Murray says he thinks this was because slaves had a way of dealing with depression, which their white owners did not. They could play the blues.

He says something else which also sounds right to me. He says the blues can't drive depression clear out of a house, but they can drive it into the corners of any room where they are being played.

I am, incidentally, honorary president of the American Humanist Association, having succeeded the late, great science-fiction writer Isaac Asimov in that utterly functionless capacity. We Humanists behave as honorably as we can without any expectations of rewards or punishments in an afterlife. We serve as best we can the only abstraction with which we have any real familiarity, which is our community.

We had a memorial service for Asimov a while back, and at one point I said, "Isaac is up in Heaven now." That was the funniest thing I could have said to an audience of Humanists. I rolled them in the aisles. It was several minutes before order could be restored.

If I should ever die, again God forbid, I hope some of you will say, "Kurt's up in Heaven now." That's my favorite joke.

How do Humanists feel about Jesus? If what he said was superb, how can it matter whether he was God or not?

When you get to my age, if you get to my age, and if you have reproduced, you will find yourself

asking your own children, who are themselves middle-aged, what life is all about. I have seven kids, four of them adopted.

Most of you here are the same age as my grandchildren. They, like you, are being royally shafted and lied to by our baby boomer corporations and government.

I put my big question about life to my biological son Mark. Mark is a pediatrician, and author of a memoir entitled *The Eden Express*. It is about his crackup, straitjacket and padded cell stuff, from which he recovered sufficiently to graduate from Harvard Medical School.

Dr. Vonnegut said this to his doddering old dad: "Father, we are here to help each other get through this thing, whatever it is." So I pass that on to you. Write it down, and put it in your computer, so you can forget it.

I have to say that's a pretty good sound bite, almost as good as, "Do unto others as you would have them do unto you." A lot of people think Jesus said that, because it is so much the sort of thing Jesus liked to say. But it was actually said by

Confucius, a Chinese, five hundred years before there was that greatest and most humane of human beings, named Jesus Christ.

The Chinese also gave us, via Marco Polo, pasta and the formula for gunpowder. The Chinese were so dumb they only used gunpowder for fireworks.

And everybody was so dumb back then that nobody in either hemisphere even knew that there was another one.

We've sure come a long way since then, only seven hundred years ago. Sometimes I wish we hadn't. I hate H-bombs and *The Jerry Springer Show*.

I love science. All Humanists do. I'm particularly fond of the big bang theory. It goes like this: There was once all this nothing, and it was so much nothing that there wasn't even such a thing as nothing. And then all of a sudden there was this great big BANG, and that's where all this crap came from. Forget the Bible.

Any questions?

You know what they should put over the entrance to the Physics Department? Just that one word:

BANG!

You know what else I think? I think life is no way to treat an animal, and not just people, but pigs and chickens, too. Life just hurts too much.

Doesn't anything socialistic make you want to throw up? Like great public schools or health insurance for all?

How about Jesus's Sermon on the Mount, the Beatitudes?

Blessed are the meek,
for they shall inherit the earth.
Blessed are the merciful,
for they shall obtain mercy.
Blessed are the peacemakers,
for they shall be called the children of God, and so on.

Not exactly planks in a Republican platform.

For some reason, the most vocal Christians among us never mention the Beatitudes. But, often with tears in their eyes, they demand that the Ten Commandments be posted in public buildings. And of course that's Moses, not Jesus. I haven't heard one of them demand that the Sermon on the Mount, the Beatitudes, be posted anywhere.

"Blessed are the merciful" in a courtroom? "Blessed are the peacemakers" in the Pentagon? Give me a break!

Only kidding, but seriously: there is a tragic flaw in our precious Constitution, and I don't know what can be done to fix it. This is it: only nutcases want to be president.

This was true even in my high school. Only seriously disturbed people ran for class president.

We might have psychiatrists examine all the candidates. But who but a nutcase would want to be a psychiatrist?

But, when you stop to think about it, only a nutcase would want to be a human being, if he or she had a choice. Such treacherous, untrustworthy, lying, and greedy animals we are!

I wouldn't trust any one of you, no matter how friendly and innocent you may appear, any farther than I could throw you. Because you're human.

And for the love of God, as the Christians say, please don't trust me. I couldn't stand it.

My favorite song? It's "How Could You Believe Me When I Said I Loved You, When You Know I've Been a Liar All My Life?"

You want to know what I pray every night?

I go down on my old knees, next to my cot in the coal bin, and I pray with all my heart, "To Whom It May Concern: Couldn't you please put my soul inside a sea otter or a barn owl instead?" I would rather be a sea otter than a human being, even if there were another oil spill.

You want to know what the British mathematician and philosopher Bertrand Russell called this planet? He said it was "the Lunatic Asylum of the Universe." And he said the inmates had taken over, and we were tormenting each other and trashing the joint. And he wasn't talking about the germs or the elephants. He meant we the people.

Lord Russell lived to be almost a hundred. His dates are 1872 to 1970 AD. What does "AD" signify? That commemorates an asylum inmate who was nailed to a wooden cross by a bunch of other inmates. With him still conscious, they—no kidding—hammered spikes through his wrists and insteps, and into the wood. Then they set the cross upright, so he had to dangle up there where

even the shortest person in the crowd could see him writhing this way and that.

Can you imagine people doing such a thing to a person?

No problem. That's entertainment. Ask the devout Roman Catholic Mel Gibson, who, as an act of piety, made a fortune with a movie about how Jesus was tortured. Never mind what Jesus said.

During the reign of King Henry the Eighth, founder of the Church of England, he had a counterfeiter boiled alive in public. Show biz again.

Mel Gibson's next movie should be *The Counterfeiter*. Box office records will again be broken.

One of the few good things about modern times: If you die horribly on television, you will not have died in vain. You will have entertained us.

And what did the great British historian Edward Gibbon have to say about the human record so far? He said, "History is indeed little more than the register of the crimes, follies and misfortunes of mankind."

The same can be said about this morning's issue of *The New York Times*.

Edward Gibbon's dates? 1737 to 1794 AD.

The French Algerian writer Albert Camus, who won a Nobel Prize for Literature in 1957, wrote that "there is but one truly serious philosophical problem, and that is suicide."

So there's another barrel of laughs from literature.

Camus himself died in an automobile accident.

His dates? 1913 to 1960 AD.

Listen: All great literature is about what a bummer it is to be a human being: *Moby-Dick*, *Huckleberry Finn*, *The Red Badge of Courage*, *The Iliad* and *The Odyssey*, *Crime and Punishment*, the Bible, and *The Charge of the Light Brigade*.

But I have to say this in defense of humankind: No matter in what era in history, including the Garden of Eden, everybody just got there. And, except for the Garden of Eden, there were already all these crazy games going on, which could make you act crazy, even if you weren't crazy to begin with. Some of the games which were already going on when you got here were love and hate, Liberalism and Conservatism, automobiles and credit cards and girls' basketball.

On the subject of crazy games already going on before any of us ever got here:

If you keep up with current events in the supermarket tabloids, you know that a team of Martian anthropologists has been studying our culture for the past ten years, since our culture is the only one worth a nickel on the whole damn planet. You can forget Brazil and Argentina.

Anyway: They went back home last week, because they knew how terrible global warming was about to be. Their space vehicle wasn't a flying saucer. It was more like a flying soup tureen. And they're little all right, only six inches high. But they aren't green. They're mauve.

And their little mauve leader, by way of farewell, said in that teeny-weeny, tanny-wanny, toney-woney little voice of hers that there were two things about American culture no Martian would ever understand.

"What is it," she squeaked, "what can it possibly be about blow jobs and golf?"

Even crazier than golf, though, is modern American politics, where, thanks to TV, and for the con-

venience of TV, you can be only one of two kinds of human beings, either a Liberal or a Conservative.

Actually, this same sort of thing happened to the people of England ten generations ago, and Sir William Gilbert, of the radical team of Gilbert and Sullivan, wrote these words for a song about it back then:

> I often think it's comical
> How nature always does contrive
> That every boy and every gal,
> That's born into the world alive,
> Is either a little Liberal,
> Or a little Conservative.

Which one are you in this country, and it's practically a law of life that you have to be one or the other? If you aren't one or the other, you might as well be a doughnut.

If some of you still haven't decided, I'll make it easy for you.

If you want to take my guns away from me, and you're all for murdering fetuses, and love it when homosexuals marry each other, and want to give

them kitchen showers, and you're for the poor, you're a Liberal.

If you are against those perversions and for the rich, you're a Conservative.

What could be simpler?

A show of hands, please: How many of you are Liberals?

On the subject of homosexuality: If you really want to hurt your parents, and you don't have the nerve to be gay, the least you can do is go into the arts. And in a few minutes I'll give a lesson in creative writing.

In the meanwhile, though, I want to talk about our government's war on drugs. It's certainly a lot better than no drugs at all. It was illegal mescaline which put my son Mark into a loony bin for a little while.

But get this: The two most widely abused and addictive and destructive of all substances are both perfectly legal. One, of course is ethyl alcohol. And President George W. Bush, no less, and by his own admission, was smashed or tiddley-poo or four sheets to the wind a good deal of the time from when he was 16 until he was 41. When he was

41, he says, Jesus appeared to him, and made him knock off the sauce, stop gargling nose paint.

Other drunks have seen pink elephants.

And what the heck, he didn't make any of the big decisions, and couldn't, and wouldn't want to in any case.

All he had to do was say he would not cut and run, no matter what happened in Iraq or Afghanistan. Where in heck can you cut and run to from Crawford, Texas? Dubuque, Iowa? Spokane?

And you know why I think he was so pissed off at Arabs? They invented algebra.

Arabs also invented the numbers we use, including a symbol for nothing, which nobody else had ever had before.

You think Arabs are dumb? Try doing long division with Roman numerals.

We're spreading democracy, are we? Same way European explorers brought Christianity to the Indians, who we now call "Native Americans." There's this story about Spaniards who were about to burn a Native American alive because he had been uppity some way. And he was lashed

to the stake, about to entertain, and a Spaniard tied a cross to the end of a long stick, and he held it up so the Native American could kiss it.

And the Native American asked why he should kiss it, and the Spaniard said if he kissed it he could get into Heaven. And the Native American asked if there were Spaniards in Heaven. He was told there were, and the Native American said he certainly didn't want to go there.

How ungrateful he was! How ungrateful are the people of Baghdad.

So let's give another big tax cut to the super-rich. That'll teach Al Qaeda a lesson it won't soon forget. Hail to the Chief.

That chief and his cohorts had as little to do with democracy as those Spaniards had to do with Jesus. We the people had absolutely no say in whatever they chose to do next. In case you hadn't noticed, they cleaned out the treasury, passing it out to pals in the war and national security rackets, leaving your generation and the next one with a perfectly enormous debt which you'll be asked to repay.

Nobody let out a peep when they did that to you, because big money and TV have disconnected every burglar alarm in the Constitution: the House, the Senate, the Supreme Court and the FBI, and We the People.

About my own history of foreign substance abuse. By the grace of God or whatever, I am not an alcoholic, largely a matter of genes. I take a couple of drinks now and then, and will do it again tonight. But two is my limit. No problem.

I am of course notoriously hooked on cigarettes. I keep hoping the things will kill me. A fire at one end and a fool at the other.

And I've been a coward about heroin and cocaine and LSD and so on, afraid they might put me over the edge, and, unlike my son Mark, I might never come back again. I did smoke a joint of marijuana one time with Jerry Garcia of the Grateful Dead, just to be sociable. It didn't seem to do anything to me, one way or the other, so I never did it again.

But I'll tell you one thing: I once had a high that not even crack cocaine could match. That was when

I got my first driver's license! Look out, world, here comes Kurt Vonnegut. I'm what a car is now. I'm a hundred horsepower now, which is eleven hundred manpower, so don't mess with me. Hiya, Babe, you want a lift somewhere?

And my car back then, a Studebaker, as I recall, was powered, as are almost all means of transportation and other machinery today, and electric power plants and furnaces, by the most addictive and destructive drugs of all, which are fossil fuels, so easy to set afire.

When you got here, even when I got here, the industrialized world was already hopelessly hooked on fossil fuels, and very soon now there won't be any more of those. Cold turkey.

You've heard of "crack babies"? Those are babies who come into the world already hooked on crack because their mothers were hooked on crack. Well, we are all fossil fuel babies.

As I speak, we are burning the last whiffs and drops and chunks of fossil fuels in a binge of thermodynamic whoopee. And while we do that, our waste products continue to make the air unbreath-

able and the water undrinkable, and more and more life forms are dying because of us.

This is a university, isn't it? Isn't it OK to tell young people the truth here? I mean this isn't like TV news, is it?

And here's what I think the truth is: we are all addicts of fossil fuels in a state of denial, about to face cold turkey.

And like so many addicts about to face cold turkey, we are now committing violent crimes to get what little is left of what we're hooked on.

But relax. I've got a joke that will dispel the gloom. It's another Martian joke. This is it, and no matter what, we've still got music and our sense of humor:

There's bad news and good news tonight, my friends. The bad news is the Martians have landed in New York City and are staying at the Waldorf-Astoria.

The good news is they only eat homeless people and they pee gasoline.

Put some of that pee in a Ferrari, and you can go a hundred miles an hour. If you're a guy, you can have

babes like you can't believe. Put some in an airplane
and you can go as fast as a bullet, and drop all kinds
of crap on the Arabs below. Put some in a school bus,
it'll get the kids to and from school. Put some in a fire
engine, and it will get firemen to a fire, so they can
put the fire out. Put some in a Honda, and it'll get
you to work, and then back home again.

And wait till you hear what the Martians
poop. It's uranium. Just one of them can light
and heat every home and school and church and
business in Tacoma.

What's it like to be my age? I can't parallel park
worth a darn anymore, so please don't watch while
I try to do it. And gravity has become a lot less
friendly and manageable than it used to be.

I have also become a flaming neuter. I am
as celibate as fifty percent of the heterosexual
Roman Catholic clergy. And celibacy is no root
canal. It's so cheap and convenient. You don't
have to do or say anything afterward, because
there is no afterward.

And when my tantrum, which is what I call my
TV set, flashes boobs and smiles in my face, and

says everybody but me is going to get laid tonight,
and this is a national emergency, so I've got to rush
out and buy a car or pills, or a folding gymnasium I
can hide under my bed, I laugh like a hyena. I know
and you know that millions and millions of good
Americans, present company not excepted, are not
going to get laid tonight.

And we flaming neuters vote! So I am look-
ing forward to the day when the President of the
United States, no less, who probably isn't going
to get laid that night, declares a National Neuter
Pride Day. And out of our closets we'll come by
the millions. Shoulders squared, chins held high,
we'll go marching up Main Streets all over this
boob-crazed democracy of ours, and laughing
like hyenas.

But hey, listen: I got a letter from a sappy
woman a while back. She knew I was sappy, too,
a Franklin Roosevelt Democrat, a friend of the
working stiffs. She was about to have a baby, not
mine. She wanted to know if it was a mistake
to bring an innocent little baby into a world as
awful as this one is. I told her that what made life

almost worth living for me was the saints I met.
These were people who behaved compassionately
and capably, no matter what, and they could
be anywhere.

So maybe some of you tonight are or may become
saints for her child to meet. Most of us are loaded
with Original Sin. But a surprising number of us,
not me, God knows, are loaded with Original Vir-
tue. Ain't that sweet?

So now it's time for me to teach creative writing.

First rule: Do not use semicolons. They are trans-
vestite hermaphrodites, representing nothing. All
they do is show you've been to college.

And I realize that some of you may be having
trouble deciding whether I am kidding or not. So
from now on I will thumb my nose at you when
I'm kidding.

For instance? Join the National Guard or the
Marines and teach democracy. (NOSE)

If I give you the finger, (FINGER) it means
Spokane is about to be attacked by Al Qaeda. In
that case wave flags, if you have them. That always
seems to scare them away. Please don't get the two

signals mixed up, or you might accidentally start World War III.

I will now exit while *The Blue Danube* comes over the PA system. Please waltz out as you leave.

6
DON'T DESPAIR IF YOU NEVER WENT TO COLLEGE!

On receiving the Carl Sandburg Award, Chicago, Illinois, October 12, 2001

The Indiana author celebrates some self-taught Midwesterners who made waves from sea to shining sea. As a young man, Vonnegut once considered becoming a labor organizer, and he admired and honored those who fought for the rights of wage earners everywhere. As a member of PEN International, he fought for the rights of writers around the world.[5]

We are America's Great Lakes people, her freshwater people, not an oceanic but a continental people. Whenever I swim in an ocean, I feel as though I am swimming in chicken soup.

5 The Carl Sandburg Literary Award, given by the Chicago Public Library Foundation, "honors an author whose significant body of work has enhanced the public's awareness of the written word."

I thank you for this honor, although it is a reminder that I am not nearly the passionate and effective artist Carl Sandburg was. And we are surely grateful for his fog which came in on little cat feet.[6] But tonight seems an apt occasion as well for celebrating what he and other American socialists did during the first half of the past century, with art, with eloquence, with organizing skills, to elevate the self-respect, the dignity, and political acumen of American wage earners, of our working class.

That wage earners, without social position or higher education or wealth, are of inferior intellect is surely belied by the fact that two of the most splendid writers and speakers on the deepest subjects in American history were self-taught workmen. I speak, of course, of Carl Sandburg of Illinois, and Abraham Lincoln, of Kentucky, then Indiana, and finally Illinois.

6 Carl Sandburg's poem "Fog" was memorized and recited in many grade schools—at least all over the Midwest when we were growing up. Everyone knew it at least for a while. It was a favorite to recite in school poetry contests because it was so short! Fog / The fog comes / on little cat feet. / It sits looking / over harbor and city / on silent haunches / and then moves on.—DW

Both, may I say, were continental, freshwater people like ourselves.

Hooray for our team!

I know upper-class graduates of Yale University who can't talk or write worth a nickel.

Socialism is no more an evil word than Christianity. Socialism no more prescribed Joseph Stalin and his secret police and shuttered churches than Christianity prescribed the Spanish Inquisition. Christianity and socialism alike, in fact, prescribe a society dedicated to the proposition that all men, women, and children are created equal, and should not starve.

Adolf Hitler, incidentally, was a two-fer. He named his party the National Socialists, the Nazis. Hitler also had crosses painted on his tanks and airplanes. The swastika wasn't a pagan symbol, as so many people believe. It was a working person's Christian cross, made of axes, of tools.

About Stalin's shuttered churches, and those in China today: Such suppression of religion was supposedly justified by Karl Marx's statement that "Religion is the opium of the people." Marx said

that back in 1844, when opium and opium deriva-
tives were the only effective pain killers anyone
could take. Marx himself had taken them. He was
grateful for the temporary relief they had given
him. He was simply noticing, and surely not con-
demning, the fact that religion could also be com-
forting to those in economic or social distress. It
was a casual truism, not a dictum.

When Marx wrote those words, by the way, we
hadn't even freed our slaves yet. Whom do you imagine
was more pleasing in the eyes of a merciful God back
then? Karl Marx or the United States of America?

Stalin was happy to take Marx's truism as a
decree, and Chinese tyrants as well, since it seem-
ingly empowered them to put preachers out of busi-
ness who might speak ill of them or their goals.

The statement has also entitled many in this
country to say that socialists are anti-religion, are
anti-God, and therefore absolutely loathsome.

I never met Carl Sandburg, and wish I had. I
would have been tongue-tied in the presence of
such a national treasure. I did get to know one
socialist of his generation, who was Powers Hap-

good of Indianapolis. After graduating from Harvard, he went to work as a coal miner, urging his working-class brothers to organize, in order to get better pay and safer working conditions. He also led protesters at the execution of the anarchists Nicolo Sacco and Bartolomeo Vanzetti in Massachusetts in 1927.

Another of our freshwater ancestors was Eugene Victor Debs, of Terre Haute, Indiana. A former locomotive fireman, Eugene Debs ran for president of the United States four times, the fourth time in 1920, when he was in prison. He said, "As long as there is a lower class, I'm in it. As long as there is a criminal element, I'm of it. As long as there's a soul in prison, I am not free." Some platform.

A paraphrase of the Beatitudes.

And again: hooray for our team.

And our own beloved Carl Sandburg had this to say about the fire-belching evangelist Billy Sunday:

You come along—tearing your shirt—yelling about Jesus.
I want to know what the hell you know about Jesus.
 Jesus had a way of talking soft, and everybody except

a few bankers and higher-ups among the con men of Jerusalem liked to have Jesus around because he never made any fake passes, and he helped the sick and gave people hope.

You come along calling us all damn fools—so fierce the froth of your own spit slobbers over your lips—always blabbering we're all going to hell straight off and you know all about it.

I've read Jesus's words. I know what he said. You don't throw any scare into me. I've got your number. I know how much you know about Jesus.

You tell people living in shanties Jesus is going to fix it up all right with them by giving them mansions in the skies after they're dead and the worms have eaten 'em.

You tell $6-a-week department store girls all they need is Jesus. You take a steel trust wop, dead without having lived, gray and shrunken at forty years of age, and you tell him to look at Jesus on the cross and he'll be all right.

You tell poor people they don't need any more money on pay day, and even if it's fierce to be out of a job, Jesus'll fix that all right, all right—all they gotta do is take Jesus the way you say.

Jesus played it different. The bankers and corporation lawyers of Jerusalem got their murderers to go after Jesus because Jesus wouldn't play their game.

I don't want a lot of gab from a bunkshooter in my religion.

Hooray for our team.

And I now take advantage of your hospitality by declaring myself a child of the Chicago Renaissance, powerfully humanized not only by Carl Sandburg, but by Edgar Lee Masters and Jane Addams and Louis Sullivan and Lake Michigan, and on and on.

And I propose a toast to an individual who wasn't an artist or working stiff of any description. She wasn't even a human being. Ladies and gentlemen of Chicago, I give you Mrs. O'Leary's cow.[7]

7 Mrs. O'Leary's cow is credited in folklore for kicking over a lantern in a barn and starting the Great Chicago Fire of 1871, which was followed by large-scale reconstruction that led to new economic and population growth.

7
WHAT THE "GHOST DANCE" OF THE NATIVE AMERICANS AND THE FRENCH PAINTERS WHO LED THE CUBIST MOVEMENT HAVE IN COMMON

The University of Chicago, Chicago, Illinois,
February 17, 1994

In which Vonnegut tells how his own fiction writing was inspired by the professor who was "low man on the totem pole" in the University of Chicago Anthropology Department.

A young woman told me a couple of years ago that she had applied for admission here. The man who interviewed her asked her why she had found the place attractive. She said it was because Philip Roth and I had both gone here, along with many other considerations, of course. He replied that Philip and I were precisely the sorts of persons who

never should have gone here. What could he have meant by that? If he is in this audience, I would appreciate meeting and talking to him afterward. I came here in 1946, immediately following my participation in a war. It was the Second World War, a name and event worthy of H. G. Wells. That war ended with our dropping atomic bombs on the civilians, and their pets and house plants, of Hiroshima and Nagasaki, quite a surprise to one and all. That such bombs were possible was first demonstrated in the abandoned football stadium of this very university, where the importance of contact sports had been discounted. The university president at that time, Robert Maynard Hutchins, was famous for saying that, whenever he felt in need of exercise, he lay down until the feeling passed. He finally wound up in a California think tank.

So far as I know, the only Second World War weapon worth a nickel to come out of Harvard, which thinks it's such hot stuff, was Napalm or jellied gasoline.

I came here from Indianapolis. In those days, that was like a provincial Frenchman's com-

ing to Paris, or an Austrian bumpkin's coming
to Vienna, or, as in the case of Adolf Hitler, to
Munich, Germany.

In those days, thanks again to Robert Maynard
Hutchins, the undergraduate course consisted of
only two years devoted to a study of the so-called
Great Books. Philip Roth is a product of that short
course. We would not meet until many years after-
ward. The graduate school was everything past
what would have been the sophomore year at other
American institutions. Like many returning vet-
erans with more than two years' worth of credits
from someplace else, I was admitted to this uncon-
ventional graduate school, with three or four years
to go before qualifying for an MA.

The credits I brought with me were near-flunks
in chemistry, physics, math, and biology. I had
actually twice flunked a course whose purpose is
to exclude people like me from careers as scientists,
which is thermodynamics.

Despite my inability to o'er-leap the intellec-
tual barrier of thermodynamics, or pile of shit,
if you like, I still wanted to be respected as a

person who thought scientifically, who loved the truth, the whole truth, and nothing but the truth. It was obvious that only a pseudoscience was a possibility for me. Ideally, I thought, it should be a pseudoscience socially superior to astrology, meteorology, hairdressing, economics, or embalming.

The two most prominent such, then as now, were psychoanalysis and cultural anthropology. Both were based, then as now, on what had regularly sent innocent persons to the electric chair or the hot squat, which is human testimony, which is blah-blah-blah. I chose cultural anthropology. The result now stands before you.

Much has been written about the effects on institutions of higher learning of the sudden influx of veterans after my war. One thing it did was bamboozle many teachers whose authority and glamour was based on their having seen a lot more of life and the world than their students had. In seminars I would occasionally try to talk about something I had observed about human beings while a soldier, as a prisoner of war, as a family man. I had a wife and kid

then. This turned out to be very bad manners, like coming to a crap game with loaded dice. No fair.

Also: we were so innocent.

In retrospect, my trying to become a member of the anthropology department was like visiting a kibbutz, a kibbutz as described by Bruno Bettelheim in *The Children of the Dream*. We returning veterans were mildly interesting strangers to be treated politely, with our understanding and theirs that we would soon go away again. And we did.

At about that time there appeared in the *New Yorker* a series of stories by Ludwig Bemelmans about a busboy who assisted a waiter in a grand hotel in Paris. The waiter was named Mespoulets, "my little chickens." Mespoulets's specialty was serving persons the management didn't want to come back again.

Every academic department has a sort of Mespoulets, I think. We certainly had one in the Writers Workshop at the University of Iowa when I taught there. The Mespoulets in the anthropology department in my time I will call Dr. Z, who is no longer among the living.

Dr. Z was lacking in the charm and stage presence fundamental to the reputation of a great cultural anthropologist. He was also having trouble getting published. So he was made thesis advisor for those of us the department's stars did not care to work with. He also gave a course in the summertime, when the rest of the department was on vacation or on a dig or whatever. The course could be about anything, since its real purpose was to entitle returning veterans to continue to receive living allowances from a grateful government. In order to make ends meet, I was working as a police reporter for the Chicago City News Bureau, practicing what might nowadays be called "urban anthropology."

Becoming one of Dr. Z's little chickens was one of the most fortunate things that ever happened to me, second only, perhaps, to my having been in Dresden when it was firebombed. He died a long time ago now, but many of his ideas live on with me. He died several years after I left. He was a suicide. He had great big ideas about science, about art, about religion, about evolution, and on and on, which he expressed in his cockamamie summer

course. Many of these, and surely the grandeur of his dealing with the biggest issues imaginable, are elements in my works of fiction.

I don't know if he left a suicide note. My guess is that he found it impossible to put his great big ideas on paper.

He had so many great big ideas that he gave me one for my thesis. I was a candidate for a master's degree, mind you, for the rank of Corporal in Academia. He said my dissertation should deal with the sort of leadership required if a radical change in a culture was to be effected. Why mess around?

So I did it. He told me to compare the leadership which inspired a peaceful Indian tribe to fight the United States Army, the so-called "Ghost Dance," with the leadership of the Cubists, who found brand-new things to do with surfaces and paint. He didn't say so, but he had already done this. And, thus directed, I reached a conclusion he must have reached.

But my thesis was rejected by the department, as both grandiose and non-anthropological. And I was out of time and money, and I accepted a job in what was then arguably the most prosperous and

compassionate socialist state in history, the General Electric Company in Schenectady, New York.

For whatever it may be worth, and it may be worth no more than "a pitcher of warm spit," as we used to say in the Army: The leadership of both the Ghost Dance and the Cubist movement had these elements in common:

1. A charismatic, gifted leader who described cultural changes which should be made;
2. Two or more respected citizens who testified that this leader was not a lunatic, but was well worth listening to;
3. A glib, personable explainer, who told the general public what the leader was up to, why he was so wonderful, and so on, day after day.

Turns out that such a table of organization worked pretty well for Adolf Hitler, too, and maybe for Robert Maynard Hutchins, when he turned this place inside out and upside down sixty years ago.

I was in Chicago a couple of years back on business, and visited my old department. Professor Sol

Tax was the only teacher from my time still on the
job. I asked after some of my old classmates, kib-
butzniks whose theses had been acceptable. One,
he said, was practicing urban anthropology in Bos-
ton, and I allowed as how I had worked for a couple
of years in an ad agency there.

I told him what I've told you, how much I owed
Dr. Z. I didn't comment on Z's having been low
man on the department's totem pole, the Mespou-
lets. I would be very happy, incidentally, if that
word, "Mespoulets," became a part of academic
conversations, identifying that faculty member
stuck with being mentor to all the nobodies going
nowhere. In ad agencies it is common to start out
in the mail room. On faculties it is common to start
out as a Mespoulets.

Use a new word three times in conversation, I
read in *Reader's Digest* when I was a juvenile delin-
quent, and it becomes a permanent part of your
vocabulary. Dr. Z was a Mespoulets, and died
without having risen above that rank. Sol Tax may
have been a Mespoulets at one time, but he cer-
tainly wasn't one when I got here. I find it hard to

believe that the head of the department, Dr. Robert Redfield, who made his reputation, and the department's reputation, too, with an extended essay called "The Folk Society," had ever been a Mespoulets. There: that's three times, I think.

Dr. Tax, recalling the department's dead and gone Mespoulets of long ago, said that Dr. Z had written well about the controversial Native American religion, the Peyote Cult.

So far as Dr. Tax was aware, Dr. Z hadn't done much writing since then. Only those of us who took Z's freestyle summer course were aware of the scale of the ambitions of our mentor. Each seminar, we came to realize, was an airing and testing of ideas in a chapter of a book about the human condition he was writing or planned to write. I didn't share that information with Dr. Tax, but I did ask him if he had the address of my dead mentor's longtime widow. He did.

She had long since remarried. I wrote to her, wanting to tell her how stimulating I had found her first husband, and how useful his wide-ranging speculations had been to me in my career in fiction.

I must have reminded her of utterly ghastly unhappiness which she had hoped to put behind her. We had never met, and never will meet, for there was no reply.

If there had been one, I would have asked her if he got any of his big ideas on paper, and where, if anywhere, some pages were. Ah me.

Long term, I am as indebted to the head of the department in my day, Dr. Robert Redfield, as I am to its Mespoulets. Dostoyevsky suggested that one sacred memory from childhood was perhaps the best education. I say to you that one plausible, romantic theory about humanity is perhaps the best prize you can take away from a university. And Dr. Redfield's theory of the Folk Society was that for me. It has been the starting point for my politics, such as they are.

My politics in a nutshell: let's stop giving corporations and newfangled contraptions what they need, and get back to giving human beings what we need.

Long before I got here, all theories of cultural evolution had been proposed and discarded, for

want of evidence to support them. Cultures were not describable, predictable rungs on a ladder societies were bound to climb, from polytheism to monotheism, for example, and so on.

But Dr. Redfield said, in effect, and I condense and paraphrase or worse: "Wait a minute. I think I can describe in some detail one stage many, many societies have reached or left behind, neither higher or lower than any other." It might be worth thinking about because it was or had been so common. Dr. Redfield's course in the Folk Society, which he gave every year, was enormously popular, drawing auditors from all over the university. Is his theory much discussed here or anywhere nowadays?

A Folk Society, he said, was a relatively small number of persons bonded by kinship and a common history of some duration, with a territory uncontested or easily defended, and sufficiently isolated so as to be little influenced by the cultures of other societies.

There can't be many such societies nowadays. There were still quite a few when I first came here. I recall the testimony of some people who had lived

in one to the effect that the isolation, the like-mind-edness, the routines and so on were suffocating.

I can believe it. I myself never visited one, unless you want to count the anthropology department itself.

But I had certainly read about a lot of them in the library here. It seemed to me that they, because of their simplicity and isolation, might be regarded as petri dishes in which human beings might demonstrate certain apparently basic human needs other than food, shelter, clothing, and sex. For want of a better word, I will call such needs spiritual, by which I mean only that they are invisible, un-smell-able, inaudible, intangible, and inedible.

Was it possible, I wondered, that certain features common to all of them not only revealed spiritual needs of all human beings, including those of us in this auditorium? Might not those features also show us methods for satisfying those needs, theatrical performances, if you will, which human beings, by their nature, can ill-afford to do without?

I think of the British Navy, whose sailors, although filling the world's oceans, felt lousy all

the time, until they started sucking limes. A vita-
min deficiency, of course! And here we are in the
post-industrial, post–Cold War whatchamacallit,
feeling lousy all the time. We get all the minerals
and vitamins we need. Is it conceivable that we are
suffering from a cultural deficiency which we can
remedy? Friends and neighbors, I say YES to that:

Let's give everybody a totem at birth. What proof
do I have that even highly educated people need
nonsensical, arbitrary symbols which will relate
them to other people and the Earth and the Uni-
verse? I am a Scorpio. Would those of you who are
also Scorpios please hold up your hands? Lookee
there! Dostoyevsky was one of us!

Yes, and let's find a way to get ourselves and others
extended families again. A husband and a wife and
some kids aren't a family, any more than a Diet Pepsi
and three Oreos is a breakfast. Twenty, thirty, forty
people—that's a family. Marriages are all busting
up. Why? Mates are saying to each other, because
they're human, "You're not enough people for me."

Yes, and let's make sure every American gets a
puberty ceremony, an impressive welcome to the

rights and duties of grown-ups. As matters now stand, only practicing Jews get those. The only way the rest of us can feel like grown-ups is to get pregnant or get somebody else pregnant or commit a felony or go to war and then come back again.

I only want to say in closing that it's nice to be home again.

IT IS HARDER
TO BE UNHAPPY
WHEN YOU
ARE EATING

CRAIG'S
ICE CREAM

8
HOW I LEARNED FROM
A TEACHER WHAT ARTISTS DO

Syracuse University, Syracuse, New York,

May 8, 1994

And how we can do it!

There are three things that I very much want to say in this brief hail and farewell. They are things which haven't been said enough to you freshly minted graduates nor to your parents or guardians, nor to me, nor to your teachers. I will say these in the body of my speech, I'm just setting you up for this.

First, I will say thank you. Second, I will say I am truly sorry—now that is the striking novelty

among the three. We live in a time when nobody
ever seems to apologize for anything; they just
weep and raise hell on the *Oprah Winfrey Show*. The
third thing I want to say to you at some point—
probably close to the end—is, "We love you." Now
if I fail to say any of those three things in the body
of this great speech, hold up your hands, and I will
remedy the deficiency.

And I'm going to ask you to hold up your hands
this early in the proceedings for another reason. I
first declare to you that the most wonderful thing,
the most valuable thing you can get from an educa-
tion is this—the memory of one person who could
really teach, whose lessons made life and yourselves
much more interesting and full of possibilities than
you had previously supposed possible. I ask this
of everyone here, including all of us up here on the
platform—How many of us, how many of you, had
such a teacher? Kindergarten counts. Please hold
up your hands. Hurry. You may want to remember
the name of that great teacher.

I thank you for being educated. There, I've
thanked you now; that way I don't have to speak to

a bunch of nincompoops. For you freshly minted college graduates, this is a puberty ceremony long overdue. We, whose principal achievement is that we are older than you, have to acknowledge at last that you are grown-ups, too. There are old poops possibly among us on this very day who will say that you are not grown-ups until you have somehow survived, as they have, some famous calamity—the Great Depression, World War II, Vietnam, whatever. Storytellers are responsible for this destructive, not to say suicidal, myth. Again and again in stories, after some terrible mess, the character is able to say at last, "Today, I am a woman; today I am a man. The end."

I apologize. I said I would apologize; I apologize now. I apologize because of the terrible mess the planet is in. But it has always been a mess. There have never been any "Good Old Days," there have just been days. And as I say to my grandchildren, "Don't look at me. I just got here myself."

So you know what I'm going to do? I declare everybody here a member of Generation A. Tomorrow is another day for all of us.

Having said that, I have made us, for a few hours at least, what most of us do not have and what we need so desperately—I have made us an extended family, one for all and all for one. A husband, a wife, and some kids is not a family; it's a terribly vulnerable survival unit. Now those of you who get married or are married, when you fight with your spouse, what each of you will be saying to the other one actually is, "You're not enough people. You're only one person. I should have hundreds of people around."

Now, I've made us an extended family. Does our family have a flag? Well, you bet. It's a big orange rectangle. Orange is a very good color and maybe the best one. It's full of vitamin C and cheerful associations, if one could forget the troubles in Ireland.

Now this gathering is a work of art. The teacher whose name I mentioned when we all remembered good teachers asked me one time, "What is it artists do?" And I mumbled something. "They do two things," he said. "First, they admit they can't straighten out the whole universe. And then sec-

ond, they make at least one little part of it exactly
as it should be. A blob of clay, a square of canvas, a
piece of paper, or whatever." We have all worked so
hard and well to make these moments and this place
exactly what it should be.

As I have told you, I had a bad uncle named Dan,
who said a male can't be a man unless he'd gone to
war. But I had a good uncle named Alex, who said,
when life was most agreeable—and it could be just
a pitcher of lemonade in the shade—he would say,
"If this isn't nice, what is?" So I say that about what
we have achieved here right now. If he hadn't said
that so regularly, maybe five or six times a month,
we might not have paused to notice how rewarding
life can be sometimes. Perhaps my good Uncle Alex
will live on in some of you members of this graduat-
ing class, if, in the future, you will pause to say out
loud every so often, "If this isn't nice, what is?"

Now, my time is up and I haven't even inspired
you with heroic tales of the past—Teddy Roosevelt's
cavalry charge up San Juan Hill, Desert Storm—
nor given you visions of a glorious future—com-
puter programs, interactive TV, the information

superhighway, speed the day. I spent too much time celebrating this very moment and place—once the future we dreamed of so long ago. This is it. We're here. How the heck did we do it?

A neighbor of mine, I hired him—he was a handyman—to build an "L" on my house where I could write. He did the whole damn thing—he built the foundation, and then the side walls and the roof. He did it all by himself. And when it was all done, he stood back and he said, "How the hell did I ever do that?" How the hell did we ever do this? We did it! And if this isn't nice, what is?

There was one thing I forgot to say, and I promised I would say, and that is, "We love you. We really do."

9
DON'T FORGET WHERE
YOU COME FROM

Butler University, Indianapolis, Indiana,
May 11, 1996

*Vonnegut celebrates his own hometown, and hopes
that some graduates will become the kind of "saints"
who make life worthwhile.*

Hello, and congratulations. And thank you. You have made our nation stronger and more admirable by becoming educated at great expense.

At great expense, God knows, God knows.

If I had it to do all over, I would choose to grow up again at Forty-fourth Street and North Illinois in Indianapolis, Indiana. I would be born again in one of this

111

city's hospitals, again be a product of its public schools.

I would again take courses in bacteriology and quantitative analysis in the summer school of Butler University.

It was all here for me, just as it has all been here for you: the best and the worst of civilization, if right here you can find music, finance, government, architecture, painting and sculpture, history, medicine, athletics, and books, books, books, and science.

And role models and teachers.

People so smart you can't believe it, and people so dumb you can't believe it.

People so nice you can't believe it, and people so mean you can't believe it.

The funniest wise man in the world when I was growing up wasn't in London or Paris or New York City. He was here in Indianapolis. His name was Kin Hubbard, and he wrote an elegant joke a day for the *Indianapolis News* under the pen name "Abe Martin."

Kin Hubbard said he didn't know anybody who'd be willing to work for what he was really worth.

He was funnier and wiser than David Letterman.

I went to high school with at least thirty people who were as funny as David Letterman.

There's something about the air here.

One woman I went to high school with, Madeline Pugh, became the head writer on the *I Love Lucy* show.

Mr. Letterman grew up here, in what show business people, which now includes our best-known politicians and so-called journalists, often call "flyover country."

We are somewhere between television cameras in Washington DC, and New York, and Los Angeles.

Please join me in saying to the undersides of their airplanes, "Go to hell."

The greatest of American presidents, Abraham Lincoln, came from Kentucky, Indiana, and Illinois.

Arguably the greatest poet and the greatest playwright of this century, T. S. Eliot and Tennessee Williams, came from St. Louis.

Arguably the greatest friend the working people in this country ever had, Eugene Debs, was from Terre Haute.

He said, "As long as there is a lower class I am in it, as long as there is a criminal class I am of it, as long as there is a soul in prison I am not free."

It used to be admirable for Americans to talk that way.

Will some educated person here tell me what went wrong?

What I'm saying is that this is very fertile soil here. I'm not talking about corn and pigs.

I'm talking about growing important souls and intellects.

The people I choose to celebrate today, though, aren't those Middle Westerners who became world famous.

Do you know, incidentally, that one of the most impossibly sophisticated, worldly persons ever to grace the planet, the composer and lyricist Cole Porter, the toast of New York and London and Paris, came from Pee-ru, Indiana?

Pee-ru, for heavens' sakes.

Can you beat it? How close is that to Brazil and Kokomo?

The people I admire the heck out of today are those who built cities like this, with universities like this one, with symphony halls like that one, with art museums like the one over there somewhere, with libraries in every neighborhood. And the churches and hospitals. And the factories and stores. Utopia.

I'm talking to TV celebrities in airplanes again:

Hey, you monstrously overpaid electronic twerps:

"Down here" is where the real lives are led.

"Down here" is where the real work gets done.

The airplane itself was invented in Ohio.

So was Alcoholics Anonymous. The rear-view mirror.

Yes, and wonderful dancers all over the world have come or will come from Butler University in Naptown. Are some of them here?

Some of you won't stay home. But please don't forget where you came from. I never did.

Notice when you're happy, and know when you've got enough.

As for throwing money at problems: that's what money is for.

My Uncle Alex Vonnegut, an insurance salesman who lived at 5033 North Pennsylvania, taught me something very important. He said that when things are going really well we should be sure to notice it. He was talking about very simple occasions, not great victories. Maybe drinking lemonade under a shade tree, or smelling the aroma of a bakery, or fishing, or listening to music coming from a concert hall while standing in the dark outside, or, dare I say, after a kiss. He told me that it was important at such times to say out loud, "If this isn't nice, what is?"

Uncle Alex, who is buried in Crown Hill along with James Whitcomb Riley, and my sister, and my parents, and my grandparents, and my great-grandparents, and John Dillinger, thought it was a terrible waste to be happy and not notice it.

So do I.

You have been called "Generation X."

You're as much Generation A as Adam and Eve were.

As I read the book of Genesis, God didn't give Adam and Eve a whole planet.

He gave them a manageable piece of property, for the sake of discussion let's say two hundred acres.

I suggest to you Adams and Eves that you set as your goals the putting of some small part of the planet into something like safe and sane and decent order.

There's a lot of cleaning up to do.

There's a lot of rebuilding to do, both spiritual and physical.

And, again, there's going to be a lot of happiness. Don't forget to notice!

UNSTUCK IN TIME—QUOTES TO PONDER

"Keep your hat on.
We may end up miles from here!"

❋

"Practicing an art, no matter how well or badly,
is a way to make your soul grow, for heaven's
sake. Sing in the shower. Dance to the radio.
Tell stories."

❋

"True terror is to wake up one morning
and discover that your high school class
is running the country."

❋

117

"A purpose of human life, no matter
who is controlling it, is to love whoever is
around to be loved."

❋

"My father was a gun nut, like Ernest
Hemingway, mainly to prove that he wasn't
effeminate, even though he was an architect and
a painter. He didn't get drunk and slug people.
Shooting animals was enough."

❋

"The good earth—we could have saved it, but
we were too damn cheap and lazy."

❋

"We have to be constantly jumping
off cliffs and developing our wings
on the way down."

❋

"You're learning that you do not inhabit a solid,
reliable social structure—that the older people
around you are worried, moody, goofy human
beings who themselves were little kids only a few
days ago. So homes can fall apart and schools
can fall apart, usually for childish reasons . . ."

❋

"Those who believe in telekinetics,
raise my hand."

❋

"When things go well for days on end,
it is a hilarious accident."

❋

"Another flaw in the human character is that
everybody wants to build and nobody wants to
maintain it."

❋

"Make love when you can.
It's good for you."

❋

"Male American artists don't even have to
shoot off guns anymore. They can even be
homosexuals, and the hell with it.
This is good."

❊

"Queer travel suggestions are
dancing lessons from God."

❊

"Humanists try to behave decently and hon-
orably without any expectation of rewards or
punishments in an afterlife. And since the cre-
ator of the universe is unknowable to us so far,
we serve as best we can the highest abstraction
of which we have some understanding, which
is our community."

❊

"Write a poem to a friend, even a lousy poem.
Do it as well as you possibly can.
You will get an enormous reward.
You will have created something."

❊

"There is only one rule that I know of, babies—,
Goddamn it, you've got to be kind."

❋

"I am enchanted by the Sermon on the Mount.
Being merciful, it seems to me, is the only good
idea we have received so far. Perhaps we will
get another good idea by and by—and then we
will have two good ideas."

❋

"A sane person in an insane society
must appear insane."

❋

"It is true that some of the characters speak
coarsely. That is because people speak coarsely in
real life. Especially soldiers and hardworking men
speak coarsely, and even our most sheltered chil-
dren know that. And we all know, too, that those
words really don't damage children much. They
didn't damage us when we were young. It was evil
deeds and lying that hurt us."

❋

"Dear future generations:
Please accept our apologies.
We were roaring drunk on petroleum."

❁

"We have mortally wounded this sweet life-sup-
porting planet—the only one in the whole Milky
Way—with a century of transportation whoopee.
Our government is conducting a war on drugs,
is it? Let them go after petroleum! Talk about
a destructive high! You put some of this stuff
in your car and you can go a hundred miles an
hour, run over the neighbor's dog, and tear the
atmosphere to smithereens."

❁

"We are dancing animals."

❁

"Hopelessness is the mother
of originality."

❁

"Librarians, not famous for their physical
strength or their powerful political connections or
their great wealth, who, all over this country, have
staunchly resisted anti-democratic bullies who
have tried to remove certain books from
their shelves, and have refused to reveal to thought
police the names of persons who
have checked out those titles."

❊

"I was a victim of a series
of accidents, as are we all."

❊

"I'm a space wanderer named Kurt."

❊

"So it goes . . ."

❊